Machines in the Home

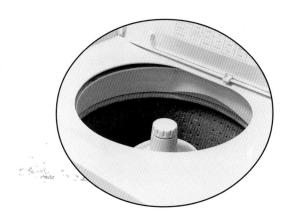

Focus: Materials

PETER SLOAN &
SHERYL SLOAN

This machine washes
clothes. It is a
washing machine.

This machine dries
clothes. It is a
clothes dryer.

This machine mixes
food. It is a
food mixer.

This machine picks
up dirt. It is a
vacuum cleaner.

This machine washes dishes. It is a dishwasher.

This machine sews cloth. It is a sewing machine.

This machine keeps food cold. It is a refrigerator.